DATE DUE

MY 28 '06		
MR 19 '07		
AP 27 '13		
DE 21 '13		
DE 21 '13		
MY 09 '15		

Demco, Inc. 38-294

THE UNITED STATES
MARINES
TODAY

THE UNITED STATES
MARINES
TODAY

KATHLEEN JAEGER

GALLERY BOOKS
An imprint of W.H. Smith Publishers Inc.
112 Madison Avenue
New York, New York 10016

A Bison Book

Published by Gallery Books
A Division of W H Smith Publishers Inc.
112 Madison Avenue
New York, New York 10016

Produced by
Bison Books Corp.
17 Sherwood Place
Greenwich, CT 06830

ISBN 0-8317-9077-6

Printed in Hong Kong

1 2 3 4 5 6 7 8 9 10

Picture Credits:

Bell Helicopter: 80 bottom.
© **George Hall:** 8-9, 15, 17, 18-19, 20-21, 22 bottom, 23, 58-59, 65, 68, 69, 70-71, 74, 76-77, 79 top, 80 top, 81, 83 top, 84-85 all, 88-89, 130 top.
Hohner, Inc: 67 bottom.

Kathleen Jaeger: 20 bottom, 86 top left.
Jack Kightlinger, The White House: 10 top.
Sgt Russell Klika, USMC: 2-3, 4-5, 7, 10 second from top, 11, 12-13, 24, 25, 26 top, 27 top, 28-29, 30 both, 31 both, 32 bottom, 33 bottom, 34-35, 36, 37, 38 top, 39 both, 40-41, 42 all, 43 both, 44-45 all, 94.
Cpl Richard Kotarba, USMC: 38 bottom.
NASA: 87.
Karl Schumacher, The White House: 86 bottom.
Pete Souza, The White House: 57-58
US Air Force: 17 bottom.
US Department of Defense: 6, 14 top, 16 top, 47, 48 both, 49, 50 top and inset, 51 both, 52-53, 54-55 all, 56 both, 57 top left and right.
US Marine Corps: 14 bottom, 16 bottom, 21 top left and right, 22 top three, 26 middle and bottom, 27 bottom left and right, 32 top, 33 top, 46, 50 bottom, 60-61 both, 62 top, 66, 67 top three, 78 bottom, 82 bottom, 90, 96.
US Navy: 20 top, 62-63 bottom, 63 top, 64 both, 72 both, 73 both, 74-75, 75 all, 78-79, 79 bottom, 82 top, 91 all.
© **Bill Yenne:** 1, 83 bottom, 86 top right, 92-93.

Acknowledgements

The author wishes to thank the following people for supplying the photographs and information to make this book possible: Major Tony Rothfork, USMC Headquarters; Ed Michalski, Department of Defense; Bob Carlisle, Department of the Navy and Sgt Russell Klika, Parris Island Recruit Depot. A special thanks to Bill Yenne for giving me the opportunity to write the book and to my Dad — once a Marine, always a Marine.

Edited by Deirdre Levenson and Carolyn Soto

Designed by Kathleen Jaeger

Page One: Marines unfurl the flag for a ceremony aboard the USS *New Jersey* commemorating the 40th anniversary of V-J Day.

Page 2-3: Bayonet techniques are part of every male Marine's training.

Below: Recruits practice to achieve the maximum score of 20 on the pull-up test.

CONTENTS

INTRODUCTION TO THE UNITED STATES MARINES

The need for both soldiers and sailors to man ships of war is ages old. Great Britain used marines with magnificent success as she set about colonizing the world, and one of those same colonies adopted a force similar to the Royal Navy and used it as a means to win independence from King George III.

The Continental Marines, which developed into the United States Marine Corps, was officially established on 10 November 1775 when Congress passed a resolution providing for two battalions of Marines to include 'good seamen or so acquainted with maritime affairs as to be able to serve with advantage by sea when required; that they be enlisted and commissioned to serve for and during the present war between Great Britain and the colonies.'

Recruitment for these first and second battalions went briskly, possibly aided by the fact that the first Marine headquarters was established in a tavern. It was at the Tun Tavern on

Opposite: Marines come ashore (using causeway) at Lebanon in May 1983.

Right: Colors are proudly displayed by recruits at the Parris Island training depot during their graduation ceremony.

King Street in Philadelphia that Samuel Nicholas, the first commandant of Marines, and Robert Mullan, owner of the tavern and a captain in the new corps, set about the task of attracting likely young men with tales of high adventure and rich bounty, all sweetened with 'one on the house.' Whether it was because of the tavern, the tales or a free drink is pure speculation, but it is fact that the nation's first naval expedition sailed on 17 February 1776 with a full complement of 268 Marines.

The Continental Marines participated in virtually all of the naval operations of the Revolutionary War, growing in number to 124 officers and 3000 enlisted men. However, after the Peace of Paris, both the Navy and Marine Corps began to dwindle in size, the latter all but disappearing. It was not until 1798, after American commerce had been plagued by French and Barbary Coast pirates, that the nation again realized its need for the Marines.

Samuel Sewall, chairman of the Congressional Naval Committee, began work on a bill to raise 'a battalion to be called the Marine Corps,' a separate service within the Navy. In July 1798 President John Adams was

Marines remain in a constant state of readiness by regularly training for all types of combat situations. Below they practice their most well known function, taking the beachhead.

Above: Commandant of Marines Paul X Kelley (right) and President Reagan.

Opposite and left: Recruits are lectured on the art of self defense, and boot camp graduates undergo an exhaustive inspection by their commanding officer.

presented with the bill, which he promptly signed into law. William Ward Burrows was then appointed commandant of the corps. Major Burrows is also remembered today as the commandant responsible for establishing the Marine Corps Band.

The mission of the Corps as described in 1798 was to perform sea duty of an amphibious nature, to serve in forts and garrisons of the United States and most significantly, to perform 'any other duty on shore, as the President, at his discretion shall direct.' The mission of today's Marine Corps has deviated little from this initial prescription, and experience from the Halls of Montezuma to the shelled streets of Beirut has taught Americans that their trust in the Marines is well placed.

The relationship of the Marine Corps to the other services has varied over the years, ranging from a small subordinate of the Navy to its present status as one of four distinct military services within the Department of Defense. Even today this statement causes occasional confusion because though the Department of Defense consists of the three Departments of the Army, Air Force and Navy, these departments are made up of the four distinct services of Army, Air Force, Navy and Marine Corps. The Marine Corps and Navy together make up the Department of the Navy with the commandant of the Marine Corps reporting directly to the secretary of the Navy. The commandant is a member of the Joint Chiefs of Staff, and in that capacity acts as one of the principal military advisors not only to the president, but to the National Security Council and to the secretary of Defense. The current commandant is General Paul X Kelley who took office on 1 July 1983, 28th in a list that includes the names Archibald Henderson and John A Lejuene.

Marines today number almost 200,000, a much smaller number than any of the other three services. How-

ever, the Marines have always professed that the smaller size only serves to prove the elite nature of the Corps. Even the slick recruitment posters advertise for just 'a few good men.' This attitude is as old as the Corps itself and is responsible in no small part for what the Marines call *esprit de corps,* that binding pride that begins in boot camp and is carried throughout a Marine's life.

Though debate over the exact organization of the Corps never seems to end, it is clear that whether in partnership with the Navy or under direct orders from the president, the Marine Corps is the nation's force-in-readiness. This constant state of preparedness is achieved by an organization aimed both at strength and flexi-

bility. The basic combat structure of the Marine Corps consists of the Marine Air-Ground Task Force (MAGTF). There are three types of MAGTFs: the Marine Amphibious Unit (MAU), the Marine Amphibious Brigade (MAB) and the Marine Amphibious Force (MAF). Each may be tailored both in size and configuration to meet a specific operational requirement. They are divided into four elements: the Command Element (CE), the Ground Combat Element

Previous page: **Drill instructors enjoy a rare quiet moment at Parris Island.**

Above: **A MAU Command Post in Lebanon.**

Opposite and right: **Marines train under freezing conditions and a paratrooper makes a reconnaissance drop.**

(GCE), the Aviation Combat Element (ACE) and the Combat Service Support Element (CSSE).

The CE allows a MAGTF to function with the kind of close integration and coordination possible only under a single commander. A MAU is commanded by a colonel, a MAB by a brigadier general and a MAF by a major general or a lieutenant general.

The GCE consists of artillery, tank, amphibious assault vehicle, reconnaissance and combat engineer units. It can range in size from a single infantry battalion to one or more divisions.

The ACE, whether consisting of a single composite helicopter squadron or several Marine Aircraft Wings may include offensive air support or air reconnaissance. An ACE can be equipped for antiair warfare, electronic warfare and to serve as command and control. The close air-ground team relationship this makes possible has always been a Marine Corps trademark.

The CSSE includes both Marine and Navy support elements. It can range in size from a single MAU Service Support Group deployed for a specific and limited mission to a MAF Service Sup-

Left: **Marines hit the beach in Lebanon in 1983.**

Below: **Under a blazing desert sun, a Marine confers with his unit.**

port Group able to provide a total range of logistic support from motor transport to dental services.

All of the above elements come together in varying sizes and configurations to make up the three types of MAGTFs, the smallest and most responsive of which is the MAU, consisting of approximately 2500 personnel. It was this type of force that the Marines deployed to Grenada during Operation *Urgent Fury* in October 1983. Today the United States continuously deploys MAUs in the Mediterranean Sea and western Pacific Ocean, and periodically in the Atlantic and Indian Oceans and the Caribbean Sea. These MAUs, in position and alert, are ready to respond to any international crisis when directed by the National Command Authority.

MAUs are normally sea based and may be deployed by amphibious ships or airlifted for a limited amount of time carrying supplies for approximately 15 days. MAUs often serve as the forward element of a MAB and consist of a Battalion Landing Team (BLT) and Composite Aircraft Squadron. The BLT is

Top: **A Marine AH-1T Cobra gunship is readied for flight.**

Right: **An Amphibious Assault Team during 'Team Spirit 85,' a joint US military forces exercise held in Korea.**

A Marine M60 tank leaves a billowing trail of dust in its wake.

reinforced by tank, antiarmor, artillery, reconnaissance, amphibious assault vehicle and combat engineer units. The MAU ACE contains four types of helicopters: CH-46 Sea Knights, CH-53 Sea Stallions, AH-1 Cobras and UH-1 Hueys. The Cobras may be replaced or reinforced by AV-8 Harrier V/STOL (Vertical/Short Takeoff and Landing) attack aircraft as the tactical situation dictates.

MABs are the next largest MAGTFs, consisting of approximately 13,000 personnel. They can be deployed for up to 30 days without resupply, and normally embark aboard as many as 20 Navy amphibious ships. MABS are capable of amphibious operations and subsequent operations ashore. The GCE is a task-organized Regimental Landing Team (RLT) consisting of two to five infantry battalions, an artillery battalion, a tank company and an anti-armor platoon. The ACE is a Marine

Left, top and bottom: **US Navy landing ships such as these are used to transport Marine troops, weapons and materiel wherever they are needed.**

Below: **A Marine jeep unit on patrol.**

Right and far right: **Troops and their vehicles deploy from helicopters, and Marines in camouflage gear descend into battle, first to fight.**

Above: **The pilot of an F/A-18 Hornet attack aircraft prepares for flight.**

Left: **A major general confers with two officers.**

Opposite top left and right: **Marines outfitted in elaborate camouflage gear.**

Opposite, top middle: **The Stinger is a man-portable antiaircraft guided missile.**

Aircraft Group (MAG) and consists of fixed-wing aircraft including AV-8 Harriers, A-4 Skyhawks, F-4 Phantoms, F/A-18 Hornets, A-6 Intruders, OV-10 Broncos and KC-130 Hercules as well as the same types of helicopters used in a MAU.

The MAF is the largest and most powerful of MAGTFs and may range in size from less than one to several divisions and aircraft wings, and include as many as 50,000 personnel. The Marine division is composed of three infantry regiments, an artillery regiment, a tank battalion, an amphibious assault vehicle battalion, a com-

bat engineer battalion and a reconnaissance battalion. The ACE is normally a Marine Aircraft Wing (MAW) which is specifically task organized for the mission. It may include as many as 650 aircraft, both fixed wing and helicopters, plus additional aircraft wings for additional combat power ashore as necessary. The MAW also includes air command and control elements with Hawk, Redeye and Stinger missile launchers.

Though these three types of MAGTFs differ greatly in size and configuration, they are each task organized for rapid deployment as part of the Navy—Marine Corps team. With timely intelligence and early deployment on amphibious ships, they can provide a continuous presence in international waters while remaining independent of established ports and airfields. MAGTFs can build quickly in size, proceed to a crisis area without revealing their exact destination and project a

selected degree of self-supporting combat power ashore. They are able to avoid the necessity to negotiate staging, transit, overflight or base rights, rent or positioning of supplies and can be rapidly withdrawn after operations, providing NCA with positive control over the level and duration of the commitment.

The organization of the MAGTFs allows for flexibility in strength, mobility and size, each of which can be precisely tailored to the specific mission assignment and assessed capability of the opposing forces. MAGTFs can operate equally well as a naval force; part of a joint task force with the Army, Navy and Air Force; as a separate service; as a combined task force with US allies; or as a joint combined task force of US forces and allies. Combined with the ability to be deployed by sealift or airlift, Marines are able to go anywhere America or her interests are endangered, quickly and efficiently.

BECOMING A UNITED STATES MARINE

Every future enlisted US Marine, whether aspiring to someday pilot an F/A-18 or guard the US embassy in Cairo, begins at the same place —the recruit depot. It is here, within minutes of debarking from the bus, that boot camp begins. Frequently described as probably the most difficult challenge a person can face short of combat, the regimen of boot camp has been successfully completed by more than half a million Americans over the past 10 years. It is extremely difficult precisely because the men who survive it may one day face combat.

The Marine Corps has two recruit training depots, one at San Diego, California and the other at Parris Island, South Carolina. Women recruits are trained only by Parris Island's Woman Recruit Training Command. Their program differs in some respects from that of the male recruits; however, the goal is the same: to build basic Marines.

Boot camp is a time of physically, mentally and psychologically demanding training. It begins with an initial period of receiving and processing. Within hours of arriving at the depot the recruit has received an introductory lecture on the Uniform Code of Military

Opposite: **A Marine recruit gives his all on the basic training circuit course.**

Above: **A recruit demonstrates the arduous skill of rappelling.**

Justice, an issue of camouflage utilities, combat boots and underwear, and for men, their first Marine Corps haircut. The close-cropped haircut endured by recruits has over the years become a symbol worn proudly by the Marine Security Guard battalion serving in embassies around the world. Recently, however, the extremely recognizable haircut is being re-evaluated for security reasons, as worldwide terrorist attacks necessitate a lower-visibility approach.

Initial processing begins with a 'contraband check.' Knives, candy, gum, radios and anything else the recruit will not need during training is tagged and put away for safekeeping. The actual processing lasts six days and consists of interviews, lectures, testing and drill. This receiving and processing stage, an intentionally low-stress period, gives way to the actual training procedure.

Marine recruit training is divided into three phases. Phase one includes the basic information and training necessary for the individual to function as a Marine and for the platoon to function as an efficient and cohesive team. It begins with an introduction to physical conditioning, close order

Above: A DI addresses his recruits.

Left and bottom: During the processing stage, newly shaven recruits are issued equipment and later take placement exams.

drill, first aid, guard duty, personal hygiene, the M16 rifle, military courtesy and discipline and Marine Corps history, customs and traditions.

Combat effectiveness depends to a great extent on the physical condition of the troops. This first phase devotes many hours to physical testing and conditioning in preparation for the physical fitness test (PFT) administered during the final training phase. By the end of phase one the platoon is beginning to look like and function as a team.

The second phase of training is dedicated to the mastery of marksmanship. The initial period is spent learning safety procedures and elementary firing techniques. Later, instructors work with members of the platoon individually to perfect firing techniques and to correct deficiencies. At the end of this training the recruits fire for record and are presented with marksmanship badges by the drill instructors. The end of phase two is called Service Week and is spent in 'mess duty' and other activities aimed at maintaining the recruit depot in a proper state of cleanliness.

Above: Close combat training includes man-to-man sessions employing the pugil stick.

Below: A recruit eyes her goal: the top of the rope.

Below: A determined recruit battles an obstacle course.

Overleaf: The circuit course is one of four rigorous courses specially designed to get recruits into prime physical condition.

Above and left: A recruit's M16 receives a thorough inspection, and an instructor offers advice during rifle training.

Opposite: M16 training, and a recruit clutches his rifle as he dodges simulated gunfire during field training.

Phase three consists of field training, the physical fitness test and the battalion commander's inspection. Field training includes offensive and defensive combat techniques, including night and day movements, field fire, as well as amphibious and helicopter assault doctrine. Since women are forbidden by law to engage in combat, they spend this time studying combat support and defensive techniques. However, weapons training is conducted.

The physical fitness test is the culmination of the intensive physical training and conditioning of boot camp. To prepare for the test, recruits run up to three miles a day, climb rope to develop arm and shoulder strength, and run a course consisting of 12 obstacles in progressive degrees of difficulty.

Marines are recognized worldwide as much by their outstanding appearance as by their fighting ability. Accordingly, one of the last hurdles a recruit must clear is the battalion commander's inspection. In preparation for this event recruits undergo meticulous uniform fittings. Equipment is examined and re-examined. Rifles,

Above: **Recruits attempt the infiltration course in a simulated combat situation.**

Left: **A dripping recruit completes a portion of the confidence course.**

slings and belts are spotless, shoes are polished and brass is shining. After passing the battalion commander's inspection, the physical fitness test and the final drill evaluation, the recruit is ready for graduation.

It is on graduation day that the recruit is addressed for the first time by the title he or she has earned — 'Marine.' After some of the toughest and most demanding training in the world, they are Marines. The Marine emblem 'Eagle, Globe and Anchor' is a part of their uniform and the Marine motto, *Semper Fidelis* (Always Faithful), a part of their lives.

After successfully completing boot camp the new Marine is ready to enter a job skill training program based on both the individual's interests and abilities as well as the needs of the Marine Corps. The program consists of formal training at Marine Corps or other service schools and on-the-job

Above: Simulated nighttime combat comes as close as possible to the real thing.

Right: Four obstacle courses test the mettle of prospective Marines.

training, and may last anywhere from a month to more than a year. Currently more than 75 percent of new Marines attend a formal school after boot camp. Available occupations range from aircraft maintenance to weather surveillance and all but those that are combat related are open to both men and women. In addition to formal training for their specific occupation, Marines are also encouraged to further their education. To this end the Marine Corps offers off-duty education programs as basic as completing a high school diploma or as complex as earning a doctorate degree. The Marine Corps will pay from 75–90 percent of tuition costs, depending on the individual's rank and time in service, and offers many financial aid programs. These policies serve to benefit the individual Marine by improving career opportunities, and the Corps by constantly upgrading the caliber of personnel.

Rappelling is only one of many skills mastered by recruits during the final and most demanding phase of basic.

Opposite and below: Graduation day. The spirit, pride and discipline these Marines acquired during the rigors of boot camp will remain with them always.

WOMEN MARINES

It would be impossible to tell the story of today's Marines without discussing the increasingly important role of the woman Marine. Walking the fine line between awareness of women's rights and traditional military thinking has not been easy for any of the services. The Marine Corps has long realized the advantage of recruiting women for service and continues to benefit from this policy.

The Marine Corps first enlisted women during World War I to perform clerical tasks and free the men in those assignments for combat duty. Opha Mae Johnson, the forerunner of today's women Marines, enlisted on 13 August 1918, just one day after the secretary of the Navy authorized the Navy and Marine Corps to accept women for service. A total of 305 women served briefly but efficiently during the war, but by 1922 all Women Reservists had returned to civilian life and the Marine Corps was again strictly a man's world.

World War II saw formation of the United States Marine Corps Women's Reserve with a recruitment slogan of 'Free a Marine to Fight,' and though

After arduous training that includes rappelling *(opposite above),* **graduation ceremonies for women Marines are particularly meaningful** *(left and opposite bottom).* **The captain at work** *(below)* **is one of over 9300 women serving in Marine noncombatant roles.**

Many recruits are surprised at the amounts of strength and stamina required to qualify in the use of the M16A2 rifle.

Top left: **A recruit in one of the four rifle firing positions.**

Middle and bottom left: **Recruits are tested on their use of the gas mask.**

met with skepticism on high at the beginning, hard work by both men and women eventually made the program a success. With a peak strength of over 19,000, almost the size of a Marine Corps division, the women reserves were told by General Alexander A Vandegrift that they could 'feel responsible for putting the 6th Marine Division in the field, for without the women filling jobs throughout the Marine Corps there would not have been sufficient men available to form that division.'

Though the line of women in the Marine Corps has been unbroken since 1942, attitudes about how they

Above: **One of the goals of the circuit course is to build upper body strength.**

Right: **A lone recruit cools down after running a demanding obstacle course.**

best serve the military mission have changed over the years and are still evolving. Today's woman Marine is assured the opportunity to advance in her career as far as her abilities will take her. A recent Woman Marine Review was conducted by the Corps to deal with questions applying specifically to the classification, assignment and deployment of enlisted women Marines. The review was convened with four objectives: to ensure commanders have sufficient men for deployment requirements; to control the combat risk for women; to guarantee equitable opportunity for men and women to serve in the Fleet Marine

Clockwise from left: **Female recruits in formation on the challenge course; in nuclear, biological and chemical warfare training and during the emblem ceremony.**

Force and the supporting establishment; and to ensure fair and equitable career progression for all Marines. Each of these objectives was dealt with and the resulting Marine Corps Order 1300.8M, published in March 1985, defines the role of enlisted women in today's Marine Corps.

One of the most striking changes concerning the role of women in the Marine Corps has to do with combat training. Beginning in October of 1985 women began studying combat techniques in response to an order by Commandant Kelley. Though women will still be excluded from units likely to engage in combat, it is felt that because of the unpredictable nature of conflicts in today's world, women may find themselves in combat situations and must be trained to protect themselves and their positions.

Combat training will consist of qualifying in the use of the M16 rifle, fighting techniques including cover, concealment and camouflage as well as how to handle grenades, mines and booby traps. Women will receive additional training in nuclear, biological and chemical defenses and the use of deadly force as a part of guard duty.

Because women will not be assigned to combat duty or to any unit likely to engage in combat, they will not be trained in offensive techniques such as the use of bayonets, combat formations, offensive techniques of fire, ship to shore movement, day or night offensive operations, patrols and ambushes and rubber boat training.

Today's woman Marine will be prepared to protect herself and her position in the event of unexpected enemy fire or terrorist attack.

UNITED STATES MARINES IN ACTION

The strength and security of the United States in today's international climate depends not only upon the ability to protect her shores but also to project a visible strength across the seas to any who would doubt her resolve. During wartime the mission is clear and the Marines are there, 'first to fight' to protect America's interests. During peacetime the mission is often less defined, yet the Marines remain stationed around the world in any potentially volatile area, using their visible strength as a deterrent while remaining ready to take any action required. In this capacity Marines have served in operations that have provided the satisfaction of a 'mission accomplished' as in Grenada and those providing only the painful frustration of undefined conflict as in Beirut.

The Marine Corps' most recent involvement in Beirut began on 25 August 1982 when 800 Marines became part of a multinational peacekeeping force with France and Italy. The force had been established to aid in the withdrawal of Israeli forces from Beirut and the evacuation of Palestine Liberation Organization (PLO) and Syrian forces. It was hoped that this

Opposite: **Marine tanks in camouflage paint schemes on desert maneuvers.**

Above: **A Marine at his post in Lebanon in 1983. During that year, Marines endured tragic losses while attempting to restore peace in the war-torn country.**

would provide the climate necessary for productive negotiations between the Israelis and Palestinians.

This was not the first time the Marines had been called on to assist in maintaining order in Lebanon. On 15 July 1958 US Marines landed south of Beirut and began to establish an armed perimeter around the city. Ordered by President Eisenhower at the request of then President Camille Chamoun, their mission was to protect the Chamoun government from a suspected *coup d'etat* by Communist forces. By the end of September some semblance of order had been restored and the Marines, praised for their restraint during the operation, left Beirut. The Mission causing them to return almost 25 years later was of a similar nature but this time the cost was tragic in its disproportion.

On 10 September 1982, the Marines returned to their ships offshore, having completed the task of evacuating Beirut. However, four days later the president of Lebanon, Bashir Gemayel, was assassinated and the Israeli Army moved back into Beirut to control the violence that seemed imminent. In a serious lapse of judgement the Israelis

allowed Christian Phalangists into Palestinian refugee camps; the resulting massacre of several hundred Palestinians by Phalangist extremists plunged the country into deeper turmoil. This prompted President Reagan on 29 September to authorize the Marines to again join the French and Italians in attempting to restore order. The Marines were given the task of guarding the Beirut International Airport, a task that was to become more difficult and costly than anyone could imagine.

One of the difficulties the Marines faced in guarding the airport resulted from being placed in a combat situation with the mission of keeping peace and not engaging in direct offensive combat. The Rules of Engagement (ROE) in Beirut were clearly spelled out and basically stated that Marines could fire back when fired upon but only when they could definitely determine that they were being *directly* fired upon and could absolutely identify a specific target. Even when these criteria were met word had to be passed up the chain of command and an answer passed back down before the Marines could return fire. Observers of this situation often described the Marines as sitting ducks.

Both pages: **The aftermath of the terrorist attack on the US embassy in Beirut on 20 September 1984. Much of the building was demolished and two US servicemen were killed.**

Below: American and Lebanese rescue workers search the destroyed building that housed Marine Headquarters in Beirut. The headquarters was the target of terrorist attack on 23 October 1983 in which 241 Marines were killed.

Inset: The body of a Marine killed in Lebanon is loaded onto a C-130.

Above: US Marines on patrol were a familiar sight for the citizens of Beirut in 1983.

Top and opposite top: Marine troops land at Landing Zone Red, and make an amphibious landing on Green Beach.

By 12 September 1983 there were 1200 Marines on shore and another 2000 on ships off the coast of Beirut. The Marines had begun to sustain casualties as a result of sniper fire, explosions and shelling. Though now authorized by the President to call in naval gunfire and air strikes if necessary to protect themselves, the essential nature of the mission remained the same and with it the same ROE. In the weeks that followed the Marines continued to exercise the restraint that they have often been praised for. This time, however, there was to be no reward and on 23 October a truck carrying 12,000 lb of explosives drove past the sentry guarding the compound where the Marines were headquartered and into the headquarters building. It was early in the morning and most of the men inside were still asleep. The resulting explosion killed 241 Marines, more than had died on any single combat action during the entire Vietnam War. Marine casualties in Beirut did not stop with the bombing. Questions about their role and presence there continued to be raised, resulting in a decision in early 1984 to withdraw all Marines from Beirut. It was a devastating time for the Marines, made worse because the nature of the mission had been so unclear and the cost so high. Still the Marines had been where they were asked to be, doing what they were asked to do, to the best of their ability.

A Marine patrols the ravaged streets of Beirut. Amid the turmoil, the Marines served with customary restraint until their withdrawal in 1984.

Fortunately not all Marine operations have been as tragic and frustrating as Beirut. A good example is the Marines' involvement in Grenada. On 25 October 1983 some 400 Marines landed on Grenada. This time US intervention was no less controversial, but the mission was clear: to rescue nearly 1000 Americans, mostly students, at St George's University School of Medicine. It was feared that because of the turmoil caused when Prime Minister Maurice Bishop and about 100 other Grenadians were killed by a group of radical leftists, the Americans were in danger of becoming political hostages. The lessons learned from a similar situation in Iran prompted a direct approach to the problem.

Operation *Urgent Fury* began before daybreak when a four-man US Navy SEAL (sea, air and land) team parachuted to a position off the southern shore. Their mission was to provide battle commanders with intelligence concerning the Cuban-built 10,000-foot runway at Point Salines, but all four of them drowned in unexpectedly high seas. Because of the rough water, Battalion Landing Team 2/8 of the 22nd MAU were ferried ashore by helicopters from the US Navy helicopter carrier USS *Guam*. They proceeded to take Pearls Airport and secure the

Above: **A disabled Marine CH-46E, abandoned on Grand Anse beach on Grenada.**

Opposite top and bottom: **A Marine LVTP-7 amphibious vehicle, and Pearls Airport, used as a receiving point on Grenada.**

northern half of the island nation meeting with very little resistance. US Army Rangers, however, parachuting onto the southern half of the island near the Point Salines airport met with stiff resistance. Cuban workers living near the airstrip were more heavily armed than the Pentagon had expected and were using antiaircraft weapons against the Rangers. However, by 7:15 the Point Salines airport area had been cleared and US Air Force C-130s were able to land. Meanwhile, the *Guam* had moved around to the west coast sending 13 amphibious vehicles with 250 Marines and five tanks to take Fort Frederick and its Richmond Hill prison near Grenada's capital of St George's. As the Marines moved down from the north toward St. George's, the Army Rangers moved up from the south. Resistance from the Grenadian revolutionaries was again much heavier than expected and by nightfall of that first long day the military had still not secured the island. By early morning the next day most of the resistance had been put down and Marines stormed

the mansion where the British governor-general was beseiged. That evening Fort Frederick and the campus of the medical school were secured and by the morning of the 27th the Atlantic Fleet commander reported that all major military objectives had been secured. It was a brief operation, but not without casualties. Eighteen Americans were killed and 67 wounded. A week later all Marines had left the island and within six weeks only about 300 US Military Police and support troops were still on Grenada. There was a job to be done, the Marines were called in, and the operation was a success.

Memorial services for the heroes of both Lebanon and Grenada were held

Above: **Pearls airport was unofficially renamed MCAS Douglas, hence the sign.**

Below: **Documents and other items found in the soldiers' barracks on Grenada.**

at Cherry Point and Camp Lejeune on 4 November 1983. President Reagan spoke for the entire country when he said: 'America seeks no new territory, nor do we wish to dominate others. Yet we commit our resources and risk the lives of those in our armed forces to rescue others from bloodshed and turmoil, and to prevent humankind from drowning in a sea of tyranny. Today, the world looks to America for leadership. And America looks to its Corps of Marines....'

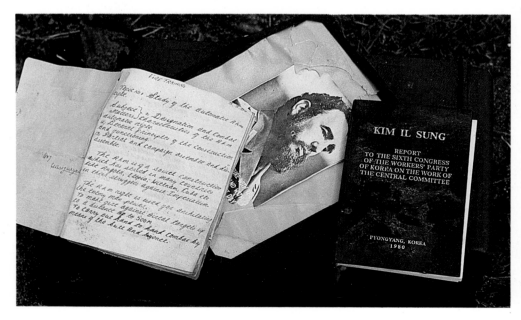

Above and left: Found on Grenada: ammo with North Korean markings, and a CH-53 about to lift a Russian antiaircraft gun.

Below: Two weeks after the headquarters bombing, Reagan discussed the tragic situation with Marines at Camp David.

AT WAR WITH TERRORISM

Operations like those in Beirut and Grenada have always been a part of the Marine Corps' mission but today Marines face a new and increasingly dangerous menace — international terrorism. In his address to Congress for fiscal year 1986, General Kelley made the Marines' role in combating terrorism a key topic, calling terrorism a new dimension in warfare that required the development of new and innovative techniques and strategies. Commandant Kelley described a seven-point program that the Marine Corps is adopting. The program is aimed at ensuring that every Marine is thoroughly aware of the terrorist threat, realistically trained and educated in how to counter the threat and armed with the best doctrine, tactics and equipment available. Efforts to provide field commanders with timely and accurate information regarding terrorist activity are being increased. Security is being tightened in order to deter terrorist attack against Marine Corps installations, facilities and deployed units.

The Marine Corps program to combat terrorism begins with coordination and monitoring of the program itself as it develops. This enables the Corps to provide centralized control at the Marine Headquarters level while establishing the agencies and working groups needed to effectively implement the measures that make up the program, monitor their success and evaluate possible improvements.

Secondly, the Marine Corps is constantly reviewing the terrorist threat and attempting to honestly assess its current capabilities to counter that threat. Since terrorism by its very nature is constantly changing, the Marines must remain capable of anticipating changes and quickly adjusting tactics, techniques, weapons and threat locations.

Intelligence, the third step, is provided by the newly established Terrorist Threat Section which interacts with other intelligence agencies addressing terrorism. This section attempts to identify specific threats to Marine Corps personnel or installations and provide timely information, recom-

Right: **Marines on maneuvers. War games are a part of a new antiterrorism program adopted by the Marine Corps. Troops are receiving extensive training to combat the threat of terrorism.**

mendations and intelligence assistance to the threatened command or region.

The fourth step being taken is to review and upgrade physical security. This includes the publication of a new security manual, acquiring new security equipment and dogs, enhancing military police training and preparing detailed security and crisis management plans.

Video tapes, films, war games, correspondence courses and mobile training teams provide some of the means to accomplish the fifth step of education. As General Kelley said during his address, 'An aware, alert, well-trained Marine is the key to defeating the terrorist.' In support of this education the

sixth part of the program provides publications on doctrine, tactics and techniques necessary for Marines and their commanders to fight the terrorist. Publications will range from policy and guidance for the commander to actual 'how to fight' techniques for the Marine on the ground facing the threat.

The final step is to enhance the ability of the Corps to operate in a terrorist environment by making certain organizational adjustments, particularly in the area of security and by establishing and publishing an operational standard to evaluate each unit's capabilities. As General Kelley told Congress, its purpose is 'to prove to enemies that terrorism is too costly a tactic to adopt against Marines.'

AMBASSADORS IN BLUE

The Marine Security Guards (MSG) are called America's Ambassadors in Blue. True to their motto, 'in every clime and place,' they are today serving in 127 detachments in 109 countries, protecting Americans abroad as Marines have been doing for over 200 years. However, they now have the added responsibility of being in the front line of the war against terrorism.

The MSG is an an elite group of nearly 1200 highly trained and lightly armed men whose job it is to guard American embassies, consulates, and legations around the world. Formally established by the Foreign Service Act

Above and right: **MSG guards in their bullet-proof monitoring stations.**

of 1946, the guard is charged by the secretary of the Navy with providing enlisted men to meet the requirements of the Department of State for security guards at Foreign Service posts.

The MSG is a strictly volunteer outfit open to male Marines in the grade of lance corporal through master sergeant. Women Marines served briefly in this post during a test period in 1979—80. Though they aquitted themselves proudly, it was decided that the potential for incidents of terrorism or other hostile action was too high, making it a combat situation.

MSG   volunteers   are   carefully

screened. They must be US citizens, and have the type of military and civilian record which will enable them to be granted a top-secret security clearance. The final requirement is that volunteers for the MSG below the rank of sergeant be unmarried. The unique situation of Post Security makes it a 24-hour mission requiring complete dedication and availability. In the event of an emergency it is felt that there would be insufficient time to secure the safety of dependents.

A Marine volunteer meeting these requirements reports to Marshall Hall, Quantico, VA for an initial training period of six weeks for sergeants and below. Senior Non-Commissioned Officers (SNCOs) train for eight weeks, the two additional weeks spent on administrative responsibilities normally assigned to an officer in any other Marine Corps assignment. After being assigned to a post, the SNCO will function as MSG commander, training NCO, administrative officer and foreign service liaison, and will be responsible to the senior American diplomat and accountable for the performance and

well-being of his detachment. This scope and latitude of responsibility is available to an SNCO only in the Marine Security Guard battalion.

MSG training is tough and much of the time is spent in a bullet-proof replica of Post #1, the access control point and monitoring station at every Marine Security Post. It is here that the Marine on guard must be able to detect even the slightest possibility of danger and remain cool and calm while responding to the situation presented. Meticulous care is given to uniforms. The trainee learns methods and procedures to ensure that his appearance is in keeping with the extremely high standards of the Guard.

Members of the Marine Security Guard battalion were in Iran to guard the embassy in 1979 and became part of what will be remembered in history as the Iranian Hostage Crisis.

Opposite: **An 'Ambassador in Blue.'**

Below and right: **The ill-fated Operation 'Evening Light' (rescue mission to Iran) gets underway. An RH-53 Sea Stallion lifts off and others prepare to follow.**

In February of 1979 Jimmy Carter began plans to send a contingent of 69 Marines and six helicopters to evacuate the 7800 Americans believed to be in Iran at the time. Before the plan could take effect however, the US embassy in Teheran was stormed. The 19-member Marine Security Guard tried to hold off the attackers by firing tear gas and later birdshot. These tactics were inadequate to deal with the magnitude of the attack and the Marines were forced to surrender. They were held with some 100 embassy employees, including Ambassador William Sullivan until representatives from the Ayatollah Khomeini arrived hours later and arranged their release. However, one Marine wounded in the attack and taken to a Teheran hospital was then kidnapped by supporters of Khomeini and held for a week before being released.

Iran continued to boil with internal unrest and to threaten the US with reprisals should any hospitality be granted Iran's deposed Shah. When President Carter finally allowed the Shah to enter the US for treatment of cancer on 22 October 1979, the pot began to boil over.

Sunday morning 4 November dawned with a mob outside the US embassy shouting 'Death to America,'

a scene the embassy personnel had become accustomed to. However, by 10:30 am demonstrators began to force the gate. The Marine guards acted with their usual restraint in holding off the mob. Their cool-headed response is credited with preventing the bloodshed it is felt would have been inevitable had they responded with fire. Thirteen Marines were among the 65 Americans taken hostage. Four black Marines and nine of the other hostages, five women and four other black men, were released two weeks later to show the terrorist's support for 'oppressed groups.' The remaining nine Marines, along with 41 other American men and two women were held in captivity for 444 days.

Since none of the appeals or negotiations to gain release of the hostages

had been successful, on 11 April 1980 President Carter ordered a military rescue mission that had been in the planning stages since early in the crisis.

Marines were members of the combined-forces team that attempted the rescue and were given the task of piloting the eight RH-53D helicopters assigned to the mission. At least six of the aging helicopters were considered essential for success and when three failed with mechanical difficulties the mission was canceled. The remaining five began to refuel from the Air Force C-130s at the rendezvous site called Desert One. During this refueling procedure, one of the helicopters collided with a C-130 and the resulting fire and explosion of ammunition caused the other helicopters to burst into flame.

Top and above: **Sea Stallion helicopters and crewmen aboard the USS *Nimitz* in preparation for the aborted hostage rescue attempt on 11 April 1980, in which these aircraft were lost and three Marines were killed.**

Opposite: **A Marine in camouflage paint.**

Eight men were killed, among them three Marines. The wounded were carried aboard the C-130s but the intense fire prevented the retrieval of the dead and their bodies were left behind. In an unprecedented act of barbarism the Iranians put the charred bodies on display at the embassy compound before finally returning them to the United States. It was to be many more months before the hostages were finally released and this episode in America's nightmare in Iran closed.

Opposite: The United States Marine Band, proud and splendid representatives of the Marine Corps spirit.

Left: Bandmaster and composer John Philip Sousa.

THE PRESIDENT'S OWN

Almost as old as the Marine Corps itself, the United States Marine Band, started by Major William Burrows, was officially established by President John Adams on 11 July 1798. Marching the streets of Philadelphia to stir up recruits for the young Corps, the band had only a few poor instruments. Major Burrows was not to be discouraged and simply assessed each officer 10 dollars to pay for needed instruments. Today the band performs over 600 concerts annually and boasts 140 pieces.

The band made its White House debut on New Year's Day 1801 and shortly after moved into the Marine barracks at Eighth and I Streets in Washington, DC, where they remain housed to this day. The Marine Band is the oldest continuously active unit in the Marine Corps.

One of the more well-known instruments of the band in former years was the Marine Band Harmonica produced by Hohner and popular with John Philip Sousa during his directorship of the Band from 1880 to 1892. The Marine Band Harmonica is still made by Hohner and is one of their more popular models, but today's more-symphonic USMC band no longer uses it in concert.

The Marine Band has played for every Presidential Inauguration since that of Thomas Jefferson, who is credited with giving the band the title 'The President's Own.'

Today's band has a number of performing ensembles, including the concert and marching bands as well as chamber orchestra, string ensembles, dance bands and a dixieland band, which tour at no expense to the taxpayer. Normally, sponsoring organizations charge an admission fee to help defray costs. Any profit made by a performance is donated to a local charity or civic project.

The United States Marine Band has seen no combat action in over 170 years. When they did it was in one of the more embarrassing actions in Marine history. Near the end of the War

Above: The Marine Band Harmonica.

Top two photos: The Marine Band during two of their many annual performances.

of 1812, members of the Marine Band joined a hastily assembled force that failed in an attempt to turn back the British, who then went on to sack the capital and burn the White House. Though the band did not go on to win fame in other battles, it has played during every war to boost the morale of the troops and civilians alike. During times of war or peace, the band continues to provide music not just for the president but for the entire country.

ARMED AND EQUIPPED TO FIGHT

Though emphasis in the USMC has always been on the quality of personnel, providing those men and women with the best materiel available is a high priority. Since the Marine mission is of an amphibious nature, one of the most important considerations is the transporting of troops and equipment from sea to land. The Marine Corps has come a long way from the row boats of 1775.

Today's state-of-the-art amphibious assault vehicle is the LCAC air-cushion landing craft which were first based at Camp Pendleton, California. The LCACs are designed primarily for amphibious assault and rapid movement of combat forces ashore, but their payload capacity of 60–75 tons and speed of 50 knots enhance the current heliborne assault capability by providing for early delivery of heavy weapons and equipment ashore. These new landing craft complement the AAVs (amphibious assault vehicles) already in use. The Marine Corps currently has 984 AAVs in use with another 327 on order. Plans for further modernization of the amphibious assault forces as well as service life extension programs (SLEPs) are expected to provide the Marine Corps with the

Opposite: **The improved semiautomatic M16A2 is the standard Marine rifle.**

Above: **The HAWK (Homing All the Way Killer) medium-range air defense missile.**

capability of simultaneous lift of both a MAB and a MAF by 1994.

Ground mobility is being increased by the delivery of a new one-and-one-quarter-ton cargo vehicle (CUCV) as well as a new five-ton tactical truck, of the M 939 series, to replace existing 2.5 and five-ton vehicles. In addition plans are underway to replace existing trucks with a new one-and-one-quarter-ton high-mobility multipurpose wheeled vehicle (HMMWV), nicknamed 'Hummer,' within the next three years.

Ground firepower and combat mobility continue to be provided by the M 60A1 Main Battle Tank with 550 currently in service. However, following successful testing, the new M1A1 was approved to begin replacing the aging M60s in fall of 1985.

The piece of equipment most essential to each Marine is still his rifle. The M16, designed in 1957 by Eugene M Stoner continues to serve the Marine Corps by providing either semiautomatic or fully automatic fire. The newly improved M16A2 version is semi- and three-round-burst automatic. It will replace the current inventory of fully automatic M16A1s by 1989.

A well-trained Marine and an up-to-date rifle are the initial building blocks

The Light Armored Vehicle (LAV) affords the Marines with a new flexibility in ground fire and maneuverability. The LAV was first fielded in 1984.

Opposite: Landing vehicles, tracked personnel (LVTP), and Marines form a 'firing line' in front of two LVTP above.

Above and right: Two LCMs aboard the USS *Vancouver*, and M48 tanks at Camp Lejeune.

of the Marine Corps, but it is the quick response and rapid deployment of thousands of Marines and tons of equipment and supplies that make the Marine Corps America's Force-in-Readiness. 1985 marked the beginning of a new program aimed at enhancing both.

The Maritime Pre-positioning Ships (MPS) concept will enable the Navy-Marine Corps team to provide a force of combined arms with 30 days of essential supplies already positioned at strategic points around the world. By the end of 1986, 13 specifically designed maritime pre-positioning ships carrying equipment and supplies sufficient for three 16,500-man brigades will be in position and ready to respond to any global crisis. Two MPS brigades were operational in 1985 and the third joined them in 1986. Construction of the cargo ships necessary to support the program has given a needed boost to the American shipbuilding industry.

The MPS program makes it possible

74

to respond to a crisis with full power in a fraction of the time it would take to transport both troops and equipment to a crisis area. Now, should the United States' interests be threatened anywhere in the world, an MPS squadron can alter course and arrive in a couple of days. Marines can then be airlifted to join their equipment and supplies on the MPS. The visibility of the MPS squadron can be controlled, allowing the US to project only the level of strength necessary to discourage a potential enemy while maintaining enough force nearby to meet with hos-

Above and above right: A Marine aims an antiaircraft gun during maneuvers, and a maritime prepositioning ship (MPS) is loaded with essential supplies.

tility should it become necessary. Each MPS squadron will take part in one Joint Chiefs of Staff-directed exercise per year.

Training exercises are the heart of the Marine Corps' ability to maintain a constant state of combat readiness. Exercises are held throughout the year and around the world. They include both Marines on active duty and Marine Reservists. It is at these mili-

Right and far right: Marines arriving in Lebanon in May of 1983: MULES bring gear ashore (right) and Marines drive an M60 down the beach shortly after landing.

tary exercises that Marines experience conditions from the frozen fjords of Norway to the sun-baked deserts of Egypt. Strategy and tactics are practiced and refined in a simulated combat atmosphere. In joint exercises with the Army, Navy and Air Force, Marines have the opportunity to practice the techniques necessary to function as part of a multiservice cohesive team.

Two AH-1T Cobra gunships reflect the dawn's early light. These attack helicopters have antiarmor capability.

Above and left: **Examples of Marine aircraft, including the CH-46F Sea Knight helicopter as it discharges troops, and the F/A-18 Hornet.**

MARINE CORPS AVIATION

From dive bombing in World War I to commanding the Space Shuttle in 1985, Marines have a proud aviation history spanning 73 years. Lt Alfred A Cunningham was assigned to the Navy's aviation camp at Annapolis, Maryland on 22 May 1912, becoming the first Marine to win his wings. By the time America entered World War I there were just 39 Marine Aviators. Because the Marines had no aircraft of their own in Europe, most of their

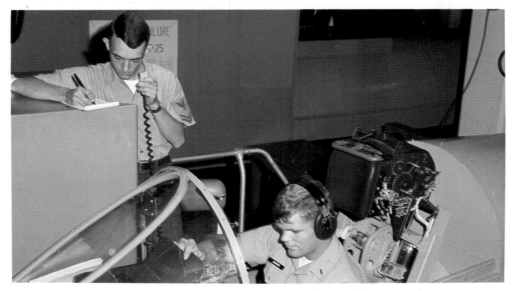

Above and right: **Flight simulators, such as these for the CH-46 helicopter and the A-6 attack plane, provide Marine aviators with invaluable training.**

flying was done with the British and French squadrons. By the end of World War I Marine Aviation had grown to nearly 2500 men.

Today there are about 4900 Marine Aviators. This is one of the careers not available to women in the Marine Corps because of the combat nature of the Marine air mission; however, women may be assigned to aviation support functions. Pilot training is available to all male commissioned officers who can meet the stringent requirements. It begins with 12 to 18

Above and left: **An EA6-B Prowler, used in electronic warfare, is serviced, and an MV-22A Osprey, which will eventually replace helicopters on many carriers.**

months at a Naval Air Training Command. The Navy trains Marine pilots and awards them Navy wings. The Navy also owns the aircraft that the Marines operate. Whether the pilots are called Naval Aviators or Marine Aviators is a subject of some debate, but there is no question that once wearing their wings and assigned to a squadron they are Marines.

The Navy has an annual budget of approximately 365 million dollars to train Navy, Marine Corps and Coast Guard pilots. All go through identical training until assignment to their individual service squadrons. The Marine Corps squadrons are jet fighters, jet attack, helicopter or multiengine transport. Marine Corps pilots fly some of the most up-to-date aircraft available and look forward to a twenty-first century that sees completion of programs now under development. One of the most exciting is the research and development of the MV-22A Osprey. This tilt-rotor aircraft will pro-

A Marine aviator poses with his F/A-18 Hornet. The Marine Corps uses the unusually versatile Hornet primarily as a fighter.

Above and left: **The Sea Stallion CH-53D, and the CH-53E Super Stallion (left), which can lift all USN and USMC fighter, attack and electronic warfare aircraft.**

vide the speed and efficiency necessary to replace the aging fleet of CH-46 helicopters by the mid-1990s. The MV-22A has been called the single greatest development in military aviation since the jet engine. Its 250-knot speed and lift capability coupled with its self-deployability and versatility far outstrip that of conventional helicopters, making it Marine Corps Aviation's highest-priority development program.

The CH-53E Super Stallion helicopter will complement the MV-22A by providing heavy-lift capability into the twenty-first century. The Super Stallion is rated at 16 tons of lift, making it capable of lifting 93 percent of all heavy equipment in a Marine Division, compared to 38 percent by its predecessor, the CH-53D Sea Stallion. In-flight refueling ability and two 650-gallon fuel tanks give the Super Stal-

Above and right: **The CH-46 Sea Knight, the principal assault helicopter for the Marine Corps. The interior is designed to accommodate personnel and supplies.**

lion an impressive range and combat capability.

In the air-to-ground and air-to-air role, the Marine Corps continues to rely on the F/A-18 Hornets. Reliable and remarkably easy to maintain, the F/A-18 completed 1984 with an 81 percent mission-capable rate and a heretofore unheard of 76 percent full-mission-capable rate. Man hours required to service the Hornet have been cut to less than half of those required to service its USMC predecessor, the F-4 Phantom.

The Marine Corps has also found the Harrier (V/STOL attack plane) to be an able complement to its fleet. The new McDonnell Douglas AV-8B Harrier II doubles the range and payload capabilities of the earlier British-built AV-8A. Funding is now being sought to upgrade the night-fighting capability of both the F/A-18 and the AV-8B,

Above and right: The AV-8A Harrier two-seat trainer and the AV-8B Harrier. Both can take off and land vertically.

Opposite, top: The A-4M Skyhawk single-seat, light-attack bomber.

as well as to provide two-seat trainer versions of the AV-8B.

The old A-6 Intruder continues to play an important role as an all-weather medium bomber. Plans to upgrade the current A-6E to A-6F include the introduction of new engines, improved radar systems and improvements aimed at increasing survivability and reliability.

Another aircraft in use in the Marine Corps since the 1950s is the A-4 Skyhawk, a single-engine, light-attack jet probably best known for its use by the US Navy's Blue Angels Squadron, a precision flying demonstration team traveling the world as 'Ambassadors of Goodwill.' Two Marine Corps pilots are currently members of this eight-man team. The Marine Corps provides transport for the Blue Angels in its own specially painted KC-130. The KC-130 is also used regularly for in-flight refueling and is affectionately called 'Fat Albert.'

One of the most important cargos transported by the Marine Aviators is the president of the United States. Sev-

eral VH-3D and VH-1N helicopters wear the title *Marine Corps One* with the designation HMX-1, and are used to carry the president from the White House lawn to a waiting US Air Force VC-137 jetliner designated *Air Force One. Marine Corps One* is also used for any short presidential junkets more appropriate to helicopter travel.

Marines have been in the air for 73 years and have now been traveling into space for 23 years. John Glenn, the first Marine in space and the first American to orbit the earth, flew the Mercury 6 mission on 20 February 1962 remaining in space for 4 hours 55 minutes and 23 seconds. Since then 12 Marines have been chosen for

NASA's astronaut program and 7 of them have already gone into space, including Colonel Robert F Overmeyer, the first Marine to command the Space Shuttle. Colonel Overmeyer was the pilot for STS-5, the first fully operational flight of the Shuttle Transportation System, which was launched from Kennedy Space Center on 11 November 1982, and commanded Space Shuttle Mission 51-B, launched on 29 April 1985. USMC Colonel Gerald P Carr is one of three astronauts holding the record for the longest time in space. Colonel Carr flew on Skylab 4 and was in space from 16 November 1973 to 8 February 1974. Colonel James F Buchli carried a bright red flag with

Top left and right: **The Blue Angels in formation, and the Marine C-130 that transports the team's equipment.**

Above: **Reagan boards** *Marine Corps One.*

Opposite: **Marine Col Robert Overmeyer commanding Space Shuttle mission 51-B.**

him when he boarded Shuttle Mission 51-C as Marine mission specialist on 23 January 1985. The flag, colors of the Commandant, was returned to General Kelley in a special ceremony. Colonel Buchli told the Commandant, 'Sir, the reason NASA picked a Marine for the mission was because we know the importance of the high ground, and you can't get any higher up than that.'

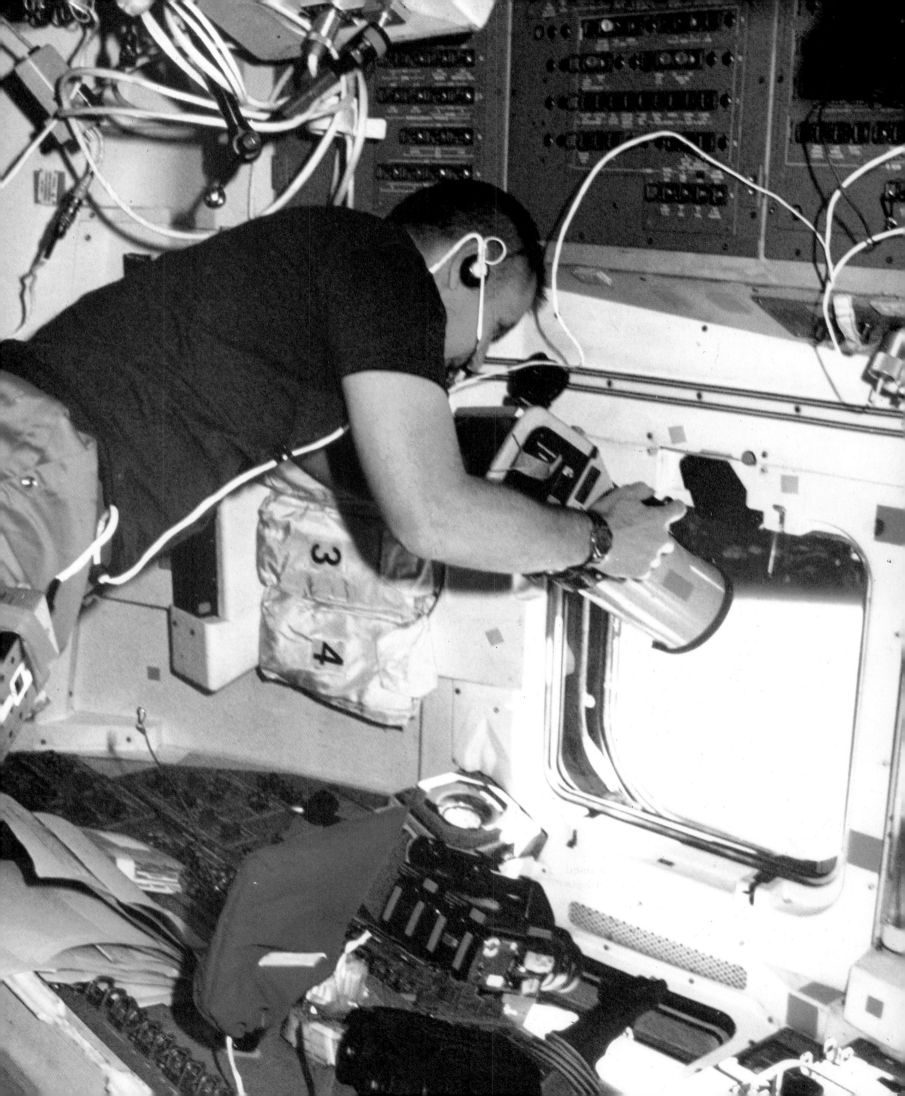

These A-4 Skyhawks are the same type of jets used by the Blue Angels, the Navy's precision flight demonstration team. Two Marines are currently Blue Angel pilots.

IN THE AIR, ON LAND AND SEA

Two hundred and ten years of pride and tradition stand behind the Marines of today. During those years the United States has always been able to rely on the Marines to go wherever they were sent and get the job done. In that service nearly 45,000 Marines have given their lives. Two hundred ninety-three Marines have earned the Medal of Honor, the nation's highest tribute. Of those, 120 lost their lives as a result of the action that earned them the medal.

What the future holds for the US Marine Corps and the nation it protects is impossible to guess. The threats we face today are certainly different from those we confronted dur-

ing the birth of our nation. Terrorism is becoming a major threat throughout the world, and because Marines have been chosen to protect our embassies and consulates abroad they are often directly in the line of fire in this most unpredictable of warfare. Recognizing this challenge, the Marine Corps is working hard to develop procedures and to train personnel to effectively fight and guard against the terrorist.

The United States remains dependent on the sea to protect our shores and to project our force around the world both as defense and as a deterrent to our enemies. The ability not only to deploy from both the sea and the air,

Opposite: **Marines in crisp dress blues.**

This page, left to right: **Marines in the field, deploying from a CH-46, and on amphibious assault maneuvers.**

A Marine makes one last call to his sweetheart before shipping out on the USS *Cayuga* in the background.

Above: **An F-4 Phantom ghosts across an eerie evening sky.**

Left: **The Marine spirit of comradeship begins in boot camp and lasts forever.**

but to maneuver rapidly and effectively once on land are trademarks of the Marine Corps. The Maritime Pre-positioning Ships program is a tremendous advance in this direction making it possible for Marines and their equipment to reach any trouble spot in a matter of days.

There is no way of knowing when or where Marines will next be called into action — but their constant state of readiness, enhanced by recent operational and equipment advances and backed by more than 200 years of practice make them worthy of the nation's trust. The Marines, *Semper Fidelis.*

INDEX

Below: Marines during operation *Ocean Venture* in Puerto Rico.

THE MARINE HYMN

From the Halls of Montezuma,
   To the shores of Tripoli;
We fight our country's battles
   In the air, on land, and sea;
First to fight for right and freedom
   and to keep our honor clean;
We are proud to claim the title of
   UNITED STATES MARINE.

Our flag's unfurled to every breeze
   From dawn to setting sun;
We have fought in every clime and place
   Where we could take a gun;
In the snow of far off northern lands
   And in sunny tropic scenes;
You will find us always on the job--
   THE UNITED STATES MARINES.

Here's health to you and to our Corps
   Which we are proud to serve;
In many a strife we've fought for life
   And never lost our nerve;
If the Army and the Navy
   Ever look on Heaven's scenes;
They will find the streets are guarded by
   UNITED STATES MARINES.